digital media positioning

Other Books by Frank Felker

The Greatest Job You Never Thought Of
*How Anyone Can Find Career Satisfaction and
Financial Independence in Sales*
Powerhouse Publishing | 2004

Recruiting Top-Producing Salespeople
*How to Attract, Retain, Manage, Compensate and Motivate
Members of the World's Most Valuable Profession*
Powerhouse Publishing | 2012

How to Build a Customer Factory for Your Small Business
Online Course
TheCustomerFactory.com
Powerhouse Publishing | 2014

Unlocking The M Cube
How to Master the Six Sides of Small Business Success
Powerhouse Publishing | 2017

digital media positioning

The Art & Science of Attracting Nothing But A-List Clients

POWER HOUSE PUBLISHING
ALEXANDRIA
VIRGINIA

Digital Media Positioning
The art & science of attracting nothing but a-list clients

by Frank Felker

Published by:
Powerhouse Publishing
625 N. Washington Street, Suite 425
Alexandria, Virginia 22314

info@powerhousepublishing.net
703-982-0984

Copyright ©2018 Frank Felker

All rights reserved. No part of this book may be reproduced in any form or by any means electronic or mechanical including but not limited to photocopying, recording, or by any information storage and retrieval system without written permission from the authors except for the inclusion of brief quotations in a review.

ISBN First Paperback Edition: 1985596172

First paperback printing February 2018
Printed in the United States of America

Felker, Frank
Digital Media Positioning, the art & science of attracting nothing but a-list clients.
1st paperback ed.

ISBN-10: 1985596172
ISBN-13: 978-1985596177

Free Resources for Readers

Thank you very much for buying this book! To show my appreciation, I have put together a bundle of bonuses for you.

- Two streaming video presentations on Digital Media Positioning (originally presented before live audiences), along with the audio tracks from both of those videos so you can listen while you drive or exercise.
- Membership in my closed Facebook group, where I offer coaching, ask-me-anything Q&A sessions and live video lessons. This group is only open to my readers and consulting clients.
- Inbox videos, audios, resources and ideas every week.
- Much, much more.

Just visit this link, register your copy
of the book and join the fun.

book.digitalmediapositioning.com

I look forward to seeing you
in the Facebook group!

Disclaimer

This book has been published for informational purposes only. Simply purchasing and reading this book will not cause you to become a recognized authority in your field. You must understand and consistently employ the precepts communicated in these pages to achieve that status.

Other free resources are available to readers in need of additional guidance by visiting book.digitalmediapositioning.com and registering their copy of the book. One of those free resources is our closed Facebook group where you can ask questions and receive answers from both the author and other members of the community.

Acknowledgements

At this point in human history, it is rare that any one person generates a truly original idea. Many people have contributed to the development of "Digital Media Positioning, the art & science of attracting nothing but A-list clients."

First and foremost, I must acknowledge the brain trust that is Jack Mize and Brian Ainsley Horn of Authority Alchemy. Jack and Brian were the first people I ever heard discuss the idea of authority positioning. The tools and processes they developed are at the center of my business. They remain my primary mentors and counselors on the topic.

Next, I want to acknowledge the contributions of my Content Marketing Brother, K. Conrad Bosmans of VAMO Media. Conrad's concept of Voice Activated Marketing is a simple, complete process for taking the spoken words of a subject matter expert and repurposing them a hundred ways to Tuesday to create an end-to-end marketing program that drives real results.

I would be remiss if I did not acknowledge the profound impact that the members of my Positive Power mastermind group have had on the development of this book. I could not have done it without you guys.

Finally, I want to recognize each of my clients. Without your brilliant messages and your faith in your ability to change lives for the better, my words and efforts would be powerless.

Dedication

This book is dedicated to Virginia Nye, my dear, sweet Honey Bunny. Without your love and support, it would have never been written.

Table of Contents

Foreword 19

Introduction 25

Chapter 1   A-List Clients 39

Chapter 2   Positioning 53

Chapter 3   Digital Media 73

Chapter 4   Positioning Yourself with Digital Media . . 81

Chapter 5   Attracting Nothing But A-list Clients
            with Digital Media Positioning 95

Conclusion 109

Afterword 113

About the Author 117

Foreword

In February of 2017, a friend and I were driving back to Washington, DC from a note investing conference in New Jersey. Throughout the conference, my friend, William Davey, had expressed surprise at how much I knew about investing in distressed mortgage notes. "You should write a book," he insisted.

The idea intrigued me. I had been involved in note investing for about four years and had put together training manuals and other materials to help hone my system. But, with three children (now four) at home and three businesses to attend to, I was sure I didn't have the time required to write a book.

William was sure I did. He knew Frank Felker well and had witnessed his method of drawing books out of authors through a series of interviews. William kept working on me and, by the time we got home from the conference, I was sold on Frank's Digital Media Positioning strategy and couldn't wait to get the process started.

I'll admit that at first, I didn't grasp the full scope of Frank's method. I understood the components of the process, but I could not have foreseen the impact their combination would have. Through our local business community, I had also known Frank for several years, and respected his knowledge and his commitment to his craft. I wasn't quite sure what to expect, but I believed Frank would guide me through the process and deliver a quality book, so I took the leap.

Less than 90 days later, my book, *Note Investing Made Easier*, debuted as an Amazon number one bestseller. After initially publishing the book in Kindle and paperback formats, Frank also helped me produce an audiobook edition, as well as two online video courses which, like the books, are marketed on Amazon.com.

When we originally met to discuss the project, Frank emphasized how the book would become a powerful business card for me. I loved the idea of having a book as my calling card but, like many people, I also had a lifelong dream "to write a book someday." If Frank were only able to fulfill those two objectives, I would have seen the project as a complete success and considered the money well spent.

But achieving those two milestones was only the beginning. From day one, copies of my book in its various editions have been selling well on Amazon. Frank repeatedly told me, "We're not publishing this book to sell a lot of books. We're publishing a book that will sell a lot of you." As it turned out, both of those things happened.

Writing this book transformed me from being just another note investor into a recognized subject matter expert. I suddenly started getting requests to do interviews on podcasts and webinars. I was asked to moderate a panel discussion at a conference. I'm exhibiting. I'm selling workshops and mentorship programs and have generated a tremendous amount of revenue — $150,000 to be exact — in only the first seven months.

Working with Frank has been such a good investment that I'm writing a second book entitled *Secrets to Winning Government Contracts*. This book is the story of how a husband and wife (me and my wife Ruth) started a business with very little capital and a lot of drive and ambition. We worked the networks and learned the systems and processes to get into the federal government as a prime contractor. I believe this book, and the live and online courses I will be teaching on the topic, will help a lot of other small businesses around the country and around the globe to not be intimidated by the big guys. If we could do it, they can too. I am confident that this second book project will be even more profitable than my first.

Should you apply Digital Media Positioning to yourself? Absolutely.

Regardless of whether you *think* you are an expert, if you know more about your subject than your audience does, and you are willing to help them, you qualify. Remember, I was not an "expert" at note investing when I wrote *Note Investing Made Easier*. There were people who had a lot more experience than I did, and there still are.

The difference between them and me is that I was willing to organize my thoughts and share them with newcomers, so that they could avoid many of the painful and costly mistakes I made early in my journey. I consider sharing that knowledge an obligation; a duty to uplift your fellow man. But they are not the only ones who benefit. The more you give, the more you receive.

Digital Media Positioning transforms you into a bona fide expert. Bestselling Author is an accolade that will apply to you for the rest of your life. And, not only are you helping educate other people about your industry, you are also opening multiple lines of revenue for yourself for years to come. It's 100% upside. Why wouldn't you take advantage of it? What could you be doing that's better than that?

Look at the work Frank has done for me and others like me. Look at the beautiful finished products and consider the impact Digital Media Positioning has had on those authors' lives. Think about all the work that goes into achieving those results. If you still aren't sure the investment isn't worthwhile, you are not one of Frank's A-List clients.

But, if you are ready to go for it, to take the leap and fully commit, you will see the reward. Frank knows who his ideal customer is. It's someone that wants it now. They want more out of life then what they're currently getting. They want to have forward momentum on a massive level. That is Frank's A-List client.

Read this book, and if the possibilities excite you as much as they excited me, if you are ready for massive improvement in your life, then Frank Felker is your Digital Media Positioning expert.

Martin Saenz, MBA MS

#1 Bestselling Author
Note Investing Made Easier

Introduction

A-List Clients & The Law of Attraction

In late October 2017, as I prepared to hit the PUBLISH button on this, my fourth book, *Digital Media Positioning: The Art and Science of Attracting Nothing but A-List Clients,* something jumped out at me.

That something was the word "Attracting."

Though I had been working on the book for weeks, I had never before made the connection between my thesis and The Law of Attraction, though it became a blinding flash of the obvious in that moment.

The Law of Attraction
Simply put, The Law of Attraction states that whatever you focus your intention, energy and thoughts toward will manifest in your life. Adherents to The Law of Attraction often employ it with the intention of attracting love, peace of mind, wealth, spiritual growth and the like.

What I was about to share in this book was how to use The Law of Attraction to bring something entirely different, but still extremely valuable, into your life: the very best clients in the world.

Focus and intention are wonderful as far as they go. But, if all you're doing is reciting affirmations, not much is going to happen. Intention must be combined with action in order to produce results. That is what the Law of Attraction is really about— being clear about what you want and taking the actions required to get it.

My intention in this Introduction is to give you some *actionable* information that can benefit you at both the personal and business levels. I'm going to explain who A-List Clients are, what they want and how to position yourself as the obvious choice when they need to have a specific problem solved. After that it's up to you to take action.

Why A-List Clients Are Critical to Business Success

Through thousands of conversations with entrepreneurs over the past 40+ years, I have come to the conclusion that all of them went into business because they wanted something more:

- More money
- More career satisfaction
- More time freedom for family and recreation

This is their "Why." Your Why may be one or more of those three, or something else entirely. But, whatever your definition of success, the clients you choose to do business with will have more impact on you achieving it than any other single variable.

Your clients will determine how much money you're going to make — big profit or no profit. They will determine how you feel about going into work every day — blessed or stressed. And, from a time freedom standpoint, they will determine whether you are running your business, or your business is running you.

Back in the 1990s, when I was operating a storefront print shop in suburban Washington, DC, I used to say, "Business would be a whole lot easier if it weren't for all those pesky customers!"

They're always walking in the door wanting something. Can't they see I'm busy?

While that may sound like a bad approach to customer service, it turned out that I was right. The vast majority of my customers were more bother than they were worth. Literally.

The Pareto Principal

You've probably heard of the Pareto Principle, also known as the 80/20 Rule. In this application, the Pareto Principal holds that 80% of your sales, or profits, come from just 20% of your customers.

In many companies that rule can be extended to 50/10. Half of their business comes from only 10% of their customers. At the print shop, my ratio was 40/1. Just two of my 200+ customers generated 40% of my sales, and over 100% of my profits.

How could they generate over 100% of my profits? Because of all the money I was losing servicing the other 99%. Like every other retailer — and most other business owners — I foolishly agreed to do business with anyone who walked through my door.

Today I focus my attention exclusively on A-List Clients, and that single strategic decision has had a more powerful impact on both the growth of my business and the quality of my life than any other choice I have made in over four decades of entrepreneurship.

What Is An A-List Client?

The definition of an A-List Client will differ for each of us. In general, A-List Clients have three things in common:

1. They have more money than time.
2. They are willing to pay a premium price for a customized solution, tailored to their specific problem.
3. They prefer to work with subject matter experts, proven solution providers.

My A-List Client avatar is a season ed, successful business owner, professional (doctor, lawyer, accountant, architect, wealth manager), coach or consultant who has a great story to tell and message to share. But they haven't done a good job communicating their unique solution set to their A-List Target Market, causing their business to stagnate and their client list to atrophy. That's a big problem. They are looking for a solution which will quickly and permanently elevate their personal brand high above their competition, dramatically moving their business to the next level. That's my A-List Offering.

A-List Offerings

A-List Clients are attracted by A-List Offerings. An A-List Offering is a product or service that cures a big point of pain for an A-List Client.

For example, a hotel owner doesn't have time to mess around when the plumbing breaks. If guests have no hot water — or no water whatsoever — the front desk switchboard is lighting up and the answers clerks are giving are not what the guests want to hear. That is a *big* pain point that requires an immediate and effective solution for which the hotel operator is willing to pay a premium price. This is why, for plumbers who do 24/7 emergency calls, hotel owners are A-List Clients, and emergency plumbing service is an A-List Offering.

Preventing big pain is another way to fashion an A-List Offering. Preventing ransomware attacks or lawsuits targeted at A-Listers will bring in big bucks. Fixing a ransomware attack after it has occurred is an even more powerful A-List Offering, for which an even higher fee can be charged, due to the immediacy of the requirement.

Another A-List Offering is the ability to fulfill a big dream. The "pain" here is the itch the prospect wants to scratch by fulfilling that dream. It's the driving hunger they have to achieve a certain goal. It's the thing that's always right at the top of their mind.

What A-List Clients are looking for is a specific, immediate, and permanent solution. What you need to do is identify their point of pain and craft a customized solution that's directly in alignment with it.

The ability to provide that powerful solution, however, isn't enough. You also have to let your A-List target market know about it through effective marketing. Back in the 1990s, Apple's Macintosh operating system had a far superior user interface to Microsoft's Windows 3.2. But which one of them ended up with a 97% market share? Windows. Why? Microsoft had better marketing.

A-Listers vs S-Listers

This diagram shows what a perfect distribution of A-List Clients and S-List Clients would look like.

What's the S-List? Think about it.

Here's what A-List Clients have in common:

1. There is a perfect match between the problem they are suffering from and the solution you provide.

2. They're easier to please. You know what they want, and you consistently give it to them. They wouldn't even consider going with anyone else, because you are the proven solution provider;

3. As a result, they are much more profitable, not just because you charge them a higher price, but also because you have an efficient solution you perform over and over.

These are the common traits of S-List Clients:

1. They are buying a generic solution, not a customized one;
2. They're never happy. You could redo the job five times, but there's still going to be a bad review on Angie's List.
3. They expect to pay commodity pricing.

Remember:

Generic Solution = Commodity Pricing.

Customized Solution = Premium Pricing.

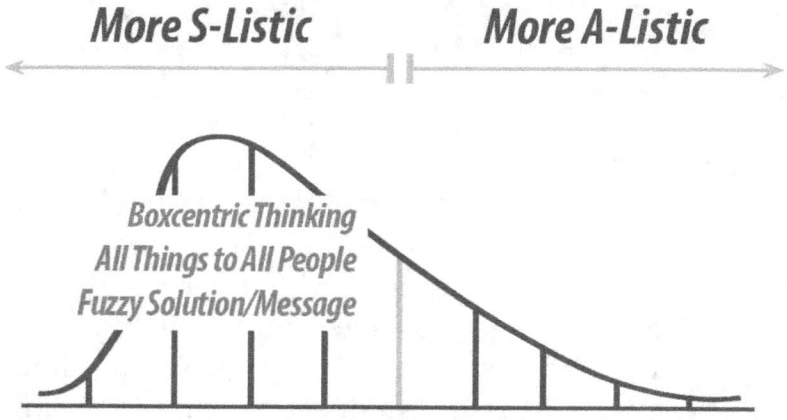

Most business owners have a client list curve that looks more like this diagram, heavily weighted to the S-List side. Why is that?

First, there are many more S-Listers out there. But there are also many reasons why you're *attracting* more of them, as opposed to the A-Listers you want.

You are guilty of thinking inside of your own "box," and not from the customer's perspective. You're focused on what you *do* instead of what your prospects *need*. J P Morgan CEO Jamie Dimon said, "The best way to look at any business is from the customer's perspective."

You are also trying to be all things to all people. Don't believe that? Consider this: If you are not currently targeting a specific client avatar, with a clear and effective solution, to an immediate and painful problem then, by definition, you are trying to be too many things for too many people. And those people aren't sure who you are, what you do, or why they should care.

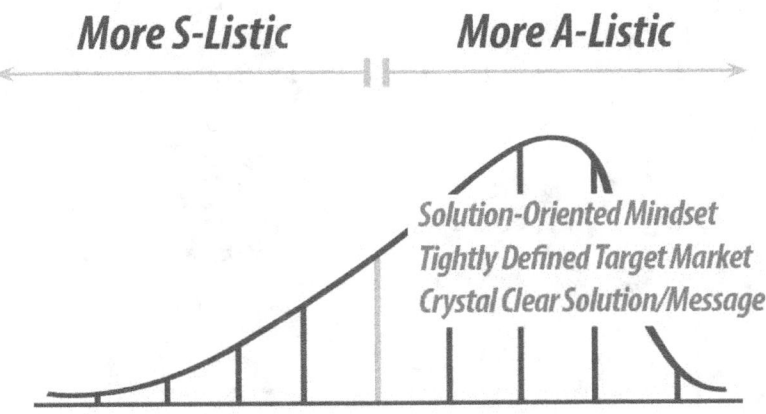

In order to have a more A-List-oriented business, like this diagram shows, you need to adopt a solution-oriented mindset, communicating a crystal-clear message to a tightly defined target market.

The Value Ladder: Nurturing A-List Clients

Not every prospective customer has the capacity to be an A-List Client — either today or in the future. But anyone who has expressed an interest in your business is a potential revenue source. You may be able to sell them a lower-priced product or service today. And you may be able to nurture and transform some lower-level clients into A-Listers over time by using something called The Value Ladder, where each step is a product or service positioned at a different price point. Now you have solution for every budget!

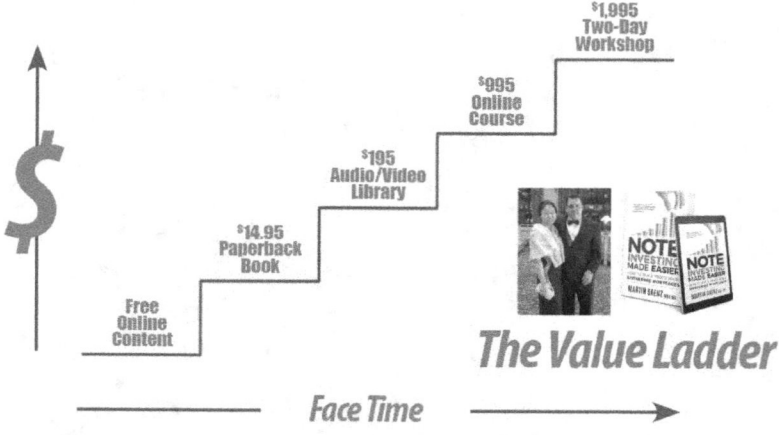

My client, Martin Saenz, is an excellent case study of the successful application of The Value Ladder.

On May 1, 2017, Martin's book, *Note Investing Made Easier,* was published in paperback and Kindle editions. It has subsequently been published as an audiobook. I put all of the editions of his book on the second step of the ladder, because it's a low-ticket product, selling for between $4.99 and $14.95.

Note Investing Made Easier debuted as an Amazon bestseller. Martin was able to leverage his new status as a bestselling author to attract people who were willing to pay $2,000 a ticket to spend two days with him at a workshop, learning how to become successful note investors themselves. By virtue of its high price point, I place Martin's workshop at the top of the ladder.

Now we are building a $1,000 online course version of his in-person workshop. Students can take the online course at their own pace, don't have to pay for travel or lodging to attend in person, and pay 50% less than live attendees. But they don't get the personal attention from or facetime with Martin, the excitement and energy of a live event, or the opportunity to network with likeminded individuals.

Although we haven't decided on it yet, I'm recommending that Martin design a $200 product in-between the book and the online course, for people who have a high level of interest in his topic but whose budget better matches that price point.

On the first step of the ladder is all the great content that Martin distributes at no charge in exchange for email registrations. He then follows up with registrants over time, in the hope that they will ascend to higher steps on the ladder as he earns their trust.

The Value Ladder accomplishes three important things for you:

1. It allows you to connect immediately with each and every prospect, wherever they are in their personal buyer's journey, maximizing your revenue opportunity.
2. Over time, it allows you to build "Know, Like and Trust" with your entire tribe, turning a certain percentage of S-Listers into A-Listers through consistent nurturing of your relationship with them.
3. It provides an upsell opportunity, no matter where your clients currently find themselves on the continuum. For example, Martin Saenz has already signed three protégés to $25,000, six-month mentoring relationships where he gives them each three full hours of dedicated personal attention every week, reviewing their deals and improving their profitability. One of his mentees, has already made a $100,000 profit on a note purchase that Martin helped him complete.

Summary of A-List Client Attraction Action Steps

Here are some simple steps you can take right away to start attracting more A-Listers:

- Think about who your favorite client is right now — someone who is easy to work with and spends the most on your services.

- Build an A-List avatar based on that person
- Mold a solution to that person's biggest problem
- Remember to think about the problem from the customer's point of view and not from yours
- Tell them about it. Create a clear marketing message that lets them know why you are the provider who understands and can solve their biggest problem
- Use The Value Ladder concept to nurture customers into increasingly valuable services or products. You should always have another level they can ascend to.

How To Use This Book

Now that you understand the premise of A-List clients, it's time to learn how to attract them to your business.

Before you begin, I want to tell that that the information in this book is presented in reverse order from the title.

In Chapter One, I define who A-List Clients are in general, and whom you should be targeting specifically.

Chapter Two is all about Positioning; what it is, why it works and how you want to be positioned in the minds of your A-List Prospects.

In Chapter Three, I talk about Digital Media; the audio, video, text, email, social posts, eBooks, printed books and live presentations you will be creating, and how to repurpose one piece of content into at least five more.

Chapter Four describes how to use all that Digital Media to position yourself as the clear choice to solve your A-List Prospects' most pressing problems.

In Chapter Five I show you how to Attract Nothing But A-List Clients using Digital Media Positioning in the four Attraction Zones: Online, Public Speaking, Networking Groups and Sales Presentations.

In the Conclusion to the book I share my strong call to action for you. I've said it before and I'll say it again: Without action, focus and intention are not only useless, they are powerless. Consider the tale of three frogs sitting on a log. One frog decides to jump off. How many frogs are left on the log? Three. Why? Because deciding to jump off a log and actually jumping off a log are two entirely different things. Jump already.

Chapter 1

A-List Clients

Find A Hole and Fill It

Henry Ford is quoted as having said, "All that is required to have a successful business is to find a hole and fill it." In other words, find a problem and solve it. Whether or not Ford is the author of this thought, the inference is correct. Problem solving is the essence of all business.

My message is that the most successful businesses are those that do the best job at solving the most vexing problems for the most profitable customers. Those businesses create A-List Offerings that are A-List Solutions to A-List Problems for A-List Clients.

Designing Your Customer

Several years ago, I created an online course entitled *How to Build A Customer Factory for Your Small Business*. In the course I presented a systematic approach any small business owner can use to manufacturer a steady stream of profitable clients. Using the illustration of a factory assembly line, I broke the process into four steps:

1. Design Your Customer

2. Pick Your Process
3. Tool It Up
4. Turn It On

Just as with automobiles, if you want to create a consistent, high-quality product with your Customer Factory, you must start with a blueprint. What does a great customer for your business look like? What do they buy? How much? How often? Where are they located? If your offering is business-to-business (B2B), what industry do they represent? How many employees do they have? What is their annual sales level?

If your offering is business-to-consumer (B2C), what is the demographic profile of your prime client avatar? Where do they live? Are they married or single? Man or woman? What are their levels of their education and income?

Clearly, there is a lot to think about. But, if you are already in business, I have a shortcut for you that will answer almost all of these questions. All you have to do is look at your list of current clients. It may well be that your top client right now defines your prime client profile. But, don't forget that there's more to it than just how much they buy from you.

Your A-List Client is also someone you really enjoy doing business with. There's no point in working with somebody that you really don't like or respect.

What I am talking about here is, in addition to who buys the most from you, who are people that you have had the most success serving? Whose needs do your solutions best match in the marketplace? Who is it that you consistently make happy as opposed to the people whose jobs always blow up? The ones you can never make happy no matter how hard you try. It's all about the A-Listers vs. the S-Listers.

Once you have identified an actual person who is your favorite customer, the next step is to create a fictional character that would be an even better customer for you. Remember, what we are doing at this stage is building an avatar, a representation of what your perfect A-List Client looks like.

Would they be just like your top customer, except they would buy more shoes than she does? Would this person buy more frequently? Would it be better if they lived closer to your location? In the B2B environment, would your best customer be in a different industry? Would they have a bigger company? How many employees do they have? What sort of growth track are they on? Are they in a mature industry or an emerging industry?

Use this exercise the way a child would; don't limit yourself when dreaming. I remember a Tony Robbins' tape I heard once. He said you should wish for things the way a child would. A child says, "I want a pony. No, I want two ponies, so my brother can have his own pony, and he won't be bugging me to ride my pony." Of course, the kid is never going to get one pony, but she still wishes for two ponies, without limits, reservations or thoughts of, "I could never make that happen." What does your two-pony A-List Client look like?

Now, let's look at it from your customer's perspective. Why is it that they like doing business with you? Is it your location? Is it your pricing? Is it your commitment to quality? Is it your fast turnaround? Is it your level of customer service? Is it your billing system? Is it the fact that they're able to do business with you online? What is it that they really like about you? Why is it that they keep buying from you? Write all of this down and think about how that magic could serve other companies like theirs.

Similarly, as you've gotten to know them better, what have you learned about them? Where are the critical pinch points within their processes? What are you able to do for them that really helps them? If it's a B2B situation, what helps you make your customer look like a hero within their company? It's all about the alignment between their pain and your solution. Define that alignment from every perspective.

Why People Hate Target Marketing

The approach I've just described — determining who your best clients are and pursuing nothing but people like them — sounds so logical that it's hard to believe more business owners don't embrace it. But the fact is that most business owners hate target marketing, and their companies suffer as a result.

The number one reason why they avoid target marketing is what I refer to as boxcentric thinking. When I was in the printing industry, all of us printers bragged to each other about the big metal boxes that we had on the floor — our printing machines. Whether a given box was an offset printing press, letterpress, silkscreen printer, digital printing device or whatever, our focus was on all of its wonderful features and functions. "Yeah, I got a 40-inch Heidelberg 6-color perfecter with UV coating and infrared dryer on backend of it. How do you like that?"

Fascinating, right?

Among us printers, these were riveting conversations. But, as I found out the hard way, my customers could not care less what kind of boxes I had or exactly how they functioned.

My expensive revelation came after I purchased a $250,000 digital printing device and was demonstrating its space age features to one of my top customers. He said, "I can see how all of that makes your job easier, but what does it mean to me?" In the coming weeks I learned that, as far as my customers were concerned, whether I had this giant box out front or a room in the back filled with monks writing on parchment paper with quill pens made no difference to them. All they cared about was that I delivered the job on time, I stuck to the price I had quoted, and the quality of the finished job was within their range of expectations. If it met those requirements, how it got done was of absolutely no consequence to them.

It's not what you do, but what they need, that matters. Stop thinking inside the box and start looking at your business from your customer's perspective.

Another reason many business owners hate the idea of target marketing is because they try to be all things to all people, which leads to being perceived as nothing by anyone.

I used to write a column for a trade magazine in the printing industry about digital printing technology, which lead manufacturers to send me prototypes and press releases regarding their latest gizmos. One day, along came a notice from a company that said they had developed a device that could literally print anything. It could print little business cards or a mural the size a building, and anything in-between, in color or black-and-white.

While being able to "print anything" sounds great from a technology standpoint, from a marketing standpoint, the device was absolutely useless. Imagine that I purchased that device for my shop and then placed an ad in the newspaper that said: "We now have a machine that can print anything. So, if you need anything, give us a call." It just doesn't add up. Buyers need a specific solution to a specific problem, not a generic solution to whatever comes along.

Another reason why business owners hate target marketing is because they are convinced that they will be leaving money on the table. "If I only target my software at podiatrists, what about all the chiropractors I could be helping?" This objection misses my point. A-List Clients don't all come from the same industry or consumer demographic. What they have in common is a painful problem and what you're targeting is a clear message about your effective, immediate and permanent solution.

Your solution may be just as effective for chiropractors as it is for podiatrists, but your messages to each must be entirely separate. You will use different words in different media to better communicate with different markets. It is critical that you target each individually, one at a time, to maximize your level of effectiveness and return on investment. Create one marketing assembly line targeting podiatrists. Test and tweak and get that sucker consistently pumping out A-List podiatrists with almost no ongoing effort from you. Then turn your attention to chiropractors and create a successful marketing process that is attracting them in droves. Lather, rinse, repeat. This is what successful business owners do.

How do you decide which marketing assembly line to build first? Look for the lowest hanging fruit. What target market can you most quickly communicate with, readily deliver value to, and have seen the most success with in the past? Go for them first. If it's chiropractors, great. Focus your marketing energies and resources at the chiropractors. While you're doing that, if a podiatrist comes flying in over the transom and lands in your lap, help him out but don't lose focus on chiropractors. Once you have one marketing assembly line up and running, move on to the next lowest hanging fruit.

If become a specialist in solving a specific problem for a given industry or a given target market and they can see that you know what you're talking about, they will buy from you. They see that you understand them, you feel their pain and, based upon third-party referrals and testimonials, they are convinced that your solution will work. No matter how tightly you niche-down, the global demand for your solution will be huge. You can make a fortune without ever having to target another vertical or create a new solution.

The Doctor-Patient Approach

Confused about how to find that A-List pain point or how to heal it? Use the approach of a doctor with a patient.

When you come to the doctor, does she start your meeting by saying, "Hey! I'm having a special on appendectomies this week! How about it?" No. The doctor asks you to describe your symptoms, then diagnoses the underlying problem and prescribes a solution that will involve one or more treatments. A good doctor is more interested in what you need than what they do.

To take the doctor-patient analogy a little further, you should see yourself as a specialist, a provider of specialized solutions, not a general practitioner. Why? Who makes more money, a primary care physician or a specialist? You visit a specialist when you have a specific problem and you are prepared to pay a premium price for the specialized solution available to them because of their specialized training and experience. That's why you go to see them and that is why you want A-List Clients to seek you out.

Examples of A-List Avatars

In the following paragraphs, I'm going to give a number of examples of A-List Avatars within a variety of industries, beginning with my own. Here are the doctor questions I ask prospective clients:

- Who do you help?
- What problem do you solve for them?
- Why do people choose you instead of an alternative solution?
- Why do you do what you do?

My A-list clients are business owners and CEOs, doctors, lawyers, coaches and consultants. They have extremely busy schedules, so they are willing to trade money for time. They are interested in buying from other professionals. They tend to make decisions quickly.

These types of clients are perfect for me, because they are willing to pay a premium price for a proven solution. They're just easier to deal with, in general, because they trust another professional's judgment and aren't going to nitpick or complain. They are also excellent referral sources.

There are many professionals I could target and lots of ways I could define what I do. But I prefer to frame myself as a specialist, and not a generalist. I don't just provide "marketing services." I am an expert in using digital media to position business professionals as authorities in their fields, allowing them to make more money in less time because they are attracting nothing but A-List Clients.

For Real Estate Agents

Residential Real Estate agents are among the worst offenders when it comes to trying to be all things to all people. When asked what would make a great referral for them, they will say, "I can help anyone buying or selling a home in the three-state area." To which my reply would be, "I don't know anyone with that problem."

There are basically three strata of agents: 1) Newbie; 2) Wannabe; 3) Top Producer. Top Producers approach their real estate agency as a business right from the start, select a specialty, invest in marketing and work like mad.

Among the specialties available to real estate agents are:

- First-time homebuyers
- Investors/Flippers
- Vacation Property Buyers/Sellers/Renters
- Neighborhood "Farms"

About 15 years ago I produced an audio program called Touch Marketing for Real Estate, where I described how successful agents target specific neighborhoods and become the local expert who handles the majority of the sales that take place there. Think about who the local expert is in your neighborhood, the one whose name and face you always see on the For Sale signs in front yards. That agent decided that you and your neighbors are his A-List and, by creating and following a specific plan, he is attracting nothing but you guys — probably in multiple neighborhoods.

For Medical Professionals

Digital media positioning for medical professionals is most effective when their area of specialty is some type of elective procedure such as cosmetic surgery,

Lasik eye surgery, gastric bypass, Invisalign or dental implants. If patients are only coming to you because you're listed in their insurance directory, it can be very hard to stand out from the crowd. And, since you're getting a steady stream of patients from the directory anyway, maybe you don't want to invest the time, trouble or treasure in Digital Media Positioning.

Following the doctor-patient approach, my medical professional clients answer questions from patients about potential outcomes, costs, risks, discomfort and recovery periods. They post articles, videos, before-and-after photos — whatever it takes to help the patient become more comfortable and better informed. Over time, the patient comes to know, like and trust the doctor, eventually choosing to move ahead with the elective procedure.

For Coaches and Consultants

As any successful coach or consultant will attest, you cannot be all things to all people and hope to succeed in their world. Specialization is a key success factor. Clients are depending upon your specific knowledge and experience to help them through the specific challenges they are facing. Some of these target specialties include:

- CEO/Entrepreneur Coach
- Sales Coach, Consultant or Trainer
- Life Coach

- Grief Counselor
- Personal Fitness Trainer
- Holistic Health Coach
- Weight Loss Coach
- You Get the Picture

Clearly, anyone who wishes to succeed as a coach must first determine who their A-List Client is and what the A-List Problem is that they are going to solve with their A-List Offering.

Conclusion

The message of this chapter comes down to focus:

- Targeted Clients
- Specific Problem
- Aligned Solution
- Clear Messaging

Many of these concepts may be foreign to you, but your ability to wrap your arms around them and put them to work will determine the level of success you will enjoy going forward.

Chapter 2

Positioning

What is Positioning?

When I speak of positioning yourself and your business, I'm using this definition: *"Positioning is an effort to influence the buyer's perception of one brand relative to another in order to occupy a clear, unique, and advantageous position in the buyer's mind."*

That simply means that Pepsi wants to be in a different place in your mind than Coke. Ford wants to be in a different place in your mind than Kia. Google wants to be in a different place in your mind than Apple. These companies are deliberately and continuously working to uniquely position their brands in all our minds.

The Sedan Example

Imagine you're looking at three similarly sized sedans. One is a Nissan Sentra, priced around $20,000. The next is a Ford Taurus priced around $32,000. And the third is a Mercedes 300 that starts at $45,000. All three are sedans, with four doors and four wheels. They will all convey four passengers successfully from Point A to Point B.

But they're all very different in terms of how they're positioned in your mind.

Which one has achieved the best positioning in the sedan market? The one that sells the most units at the most profitable price point. Which sedan should you position yourself as? The Mercedes.

What's Your Position?

Going forward, I'd like you to position yourself as the Mercedes, but how are you currently positioned in the minds of your A-List target market? You don't need to guess. From the client's perspective, professional service providers fall into one of only three different positions.

The Unknown

Your A-List prospects have never heard of you. About 15 out of 20 service providers, or 75%, fall into this group. Members of this group may be perfectly competent, relative to the services they provide. But they are clearly incompetent at marketing. I have long held that, for most business owners, marketing is a mystery and sales is a dirty word.

The Unclear

The next 4 out of those 20 providers, or about 20%, have achieved a flicker of personal brand recognition in the minds of their targeted A-List Clients. Your A-Listers may have seen your sign or bumper sticker or ad somewhere. But they're not sure if your name is Bob or Bill or if you're a plumber or a real estate agent. You have put some small amount of effort and investment into marketing, but it clearly is not working.

This means 19 out of 20 — 95% of the people in your industry have made no appreciable impact on their potential clients' awareness of them, their business or the painful problem they solve. Ask yourself honestly: are you among that 95% And, if you are, who would you identify as the five-percenter, your A-List's obvious choice?

The Obvious Choice

This is the person your A-Listers immediately think of when they have the problem that she quickly, effectively and permanently solves. Whether they need to buy some real estate, get their kids braces, or file for divorce, she is the recognized subject matter expert they immediately think of. Why? Because she has done such an excellent job of positioning herself in their minds.

Here's a quick example from the real estate industry. Gary Keller, co-founder of Keller-Williams Real Estate, wrote an outstanding book titled *The Millionaire Real Estate Agent*. In it, Keller states that, in every neighborhood, there is one — and sometimes two — real estate agent(s) who "own" that area.

You see their signs in front of virtually every property that comes up for sale in the neighborhood. They are your "Hometown Expert" due to years of successful target marketing and positioning. There are thousands of agents who are licensed to represent properties in that neighborhood (75%) that you have never heard of and never will. There are a handful of agents who get an occasional listing there (20%) but you couldn't name one of them. No, folks in that neighborhood choose to do business with those one or two agents (5%) they know, like and trust to be experts on their unique situation. It's an obvious and easy choice to make.

Personal Branding

The Brand of Lincoln

Whether we know it or not, each of us has a personal brand. Our brand is how people perceive us in the business world and society in general. Being as your brand already exists in the minds of everyone you know, it is important that you manage it proactively if you wish to achieve maximum success in business.

Here's an example of a personal brand that all Americans share in their collective consciousness. If I say the words "Abraham Lincoln" to you, certain images come to mind: a stovepipe hat, long beard, gaunt facial appearance, lanky build, "Honest Abe," born in a log cabin, etc. This is all part of his branding, whether he tried to make it that way or not.

Each of us has a story or impression that exists in the minds of others. The point I'm making is that *you need to take charge of that story*. I'm not saying you need to make it up. You already have a great story. But you must ensure that it's being expressed correctly, to the right group of people, consistently, over time.

Dan Kennedy, the internationally known marketing guru says, "If you aren't deliberately, systematically, and methodically establishing yourself as a subject matter expert, you're asleep at the wheel and ignoring what is fueling the entire economy around you." In today's world, the "economy around you" consists of the Internet, social media, video, audio, email, podcasts and online publishing platforms – what I call Digital Media.

Branding Yourself as a Subject Matter Expert

There used to be a saying, "Nobody ever got fired for hiring IBM." That was because, even though IBM charged the highest price, they were known for always taking care of your problem. Your boss might complain about they charged, but you weren't going to get fired because the job got screwed up.

A-List Clients hire IBM. They look for proven solution providers — subject matter experts – because choosing a subject matter expert is a low-risk purchase decision. They prefer to pay a premium price to get the problem solved quickly rather than paying less for a potentially unsatisfactory outcome.

How can you become that subject matter expert? Rule #1: Don't say, "I'm an expert." As soon as A-Listers hear that, they tune out and move on. Instead, I recommend you don what I call the mantel of the generous educator and sincere advocate for the success of your tribe. Freely answer their questions and solve their problems across every medium: online, video, in person, print, publicity, online courses, audio books, podcasts, and so on. Everywhere they look they should see your face, talking directly to them, one-to-one, addressing their biggest problems and providing real world solutions.

I had an audience member speak up during my last A-List Client Attraction presentation (the one that became this book). Her name is Hannah, and she works for a company that provides therapy and counseling for families with children with Autism. She was struggling to see how her business could use this idea of positioning, given that most people don't know her type of practice exists until they have a child with a problem. She generally attracts new clients only when a doctor writes a prescription for their service.

This passive approach has allowed the practice to survive, but I saw many ways Hannah could be proactive and position herself as the subject matter expert for this type of autism therapy.

Imagine how much easier it would be for the practice to get clients if, whenever parents did an Internet search on the highly specific medical terms that relate to her service, Hannah's instructional videos, courses and books came up in the search results? Imagine all the social proof and level of credibility that would create with those parents, even though they'd never met her before? They would immediately see her as the subject matter expert. The person who knows how to answer their questions and solve their problems.

I explained to Hannah that the key is to create content that matches the exact questions the parents are trying to find answers for. She can craft titles or headlines that use the specific terminology doctors use when talking about the diagnosis to parents. When a mom or dad researching that problem online sees the exact string of words the doctor said, it will jump off the screen at them. That's the goal. That's how Hannah can begin to attract A-List Clients to her practice.

As her audience grows and more and more people are getting answers they need, they will start sharing her content and referring others to her. There are a number of ways to accomplish this, but ultimately, Hannah needs to take charge of her message across multiple platforms, and the more effective she is at positioning herself as the subject matter expert, the easier it will be for her to get clients walking through the door.

Famous Examples

Dave Ramsey

Dave Ramsey is a great example of someone who became wildly successful because of how he very specifically positioned himself to his target market. As a young man in his mid-20s, Ramsey was a successful real estate investor, until federal laws on lending suddenly changed, causing him to get more than a little stretched out financially. When his loans were called in, he couldn't cover them. His business went right down the tubes, and he was forced to declare bankruptcy.

Through that experience, he made it his life's mission to learn everything there was to know about individuals getting themselves out of debt. That is an extremely targeted vertical. Individuals — not companies, non-profits, states, counties or municipalities. His message was to individuals desperate to get out of personal debt, period. He became the expert. Now everyone knows Dave Ramsey. He's a bestselling author, educator and syndicated radio host making millions every year just by sharing what he has learned to a group that is starving for the solution he provides.

Barbara Corcoran

Barbara Corcoran is now best known for her appearances on the television show *Shark Tank*. But she started out with a small real estate brokerage in Manhattan. Residential real estate on the island of Manhattan was her laser-focused target. Her eleven agents had made six residential sales in the previous six months. She calculated what the average sale was and put a report together with a headline that read, "The average cost of a piece of Manhattan real estate is...." She created a simple little photocopied newsletter called *The Corcoran Report*, printed the copies, folded them up herself, put them in envelopes, licked stamps and mailed them to every New York reporter she was aware of. One of them picked it up, and her report ran on the front page of the real estate section of the *New York Times*. The rest is history. Her willingness to share valuable information at no charge made that happen.

Gary Vaynerchuk

Gary Vaynerchuk is another positioning success story. He's now a famous Internet marketing guru. But his success began when he took over his family's $3 million wine business. He changed the name of the company and started a YouTube channel, doing an informative and fun daily video called *Wine Library TV*. Word spread, and the business grew from $3 million to $60 million in annual sales. He sold the wine store and became a full-time marketing author and educator, a venture capitalist and a reality TV star. Free, valuable information paved the way.

Everyday Examples

While Dave Ramsey and Barbara Cochran are nationally famous subject matter experts, thousands of lesser-known professionals are leveraging the same strategy and tactics to generate tens of thousands of dollars they would otherwise be leaving on the table. Here are a few examples, beginning with a story of my own.

Frank Felker

Back in the 1990s the printing industry was going through a technological revolution that had many shop owners running scared. As a bleeding-edge early innovator in digital and online technology, I knew more than most of my peers about what was going on and how to adapt and profit from the changes. I landed a monthly column on the topic in our industry's largest trade magazine and began to publish my own newsletter called *Digital Printing Trends*.

As a result, I began to be invited to industry conferences to give seminars. At the conclusion of one such seminar, in front of several hundred business owners, I closed by saying, "I'll take $100 of the regular annual subscription cost of my newsletter to anyone present today. Just see me in the back of the room to get a full 12 months of *Digital Printing Trends* for just $197."

It was just little ole' me in the back, signing people up by hand. People came in droves to get their subscription, paying by cash, check and credit card numbers scribbled on scraps of paper. Who knows how many more I could have sold if I had had the foresight to bring someone with me to help process the orders. Many people waiting in line gave up and went on to lunch. Nonetheless, I ended up selling over 70 newsletter subscriptions from that one talk, which amounted to over $14,000 in revenue from a single 90-minute presentation.

Martin Saenz

Martin came to me in February 2017 saying he wanted help writing a book to position himself as an expert in the mortgage note-investing world. We did just that. Because his book, *Note Investing Made Easier*, debuted as an Amazon #1 bestseller, he now runs two-day note investing workshops around the country, where he commands $2,000 per ticket. He also charges $25,000 for six months of hands-on mentoring. His book is now available in paperback, Kindle and audiobook editions and we are just about to publish an online version of his two-day live workshop. Between book sales, workshops and mentoring, Martin generated over $100,000 in the first six months after his book was published.

Conrad Bosmans

This is a short story, but still sweet. A friend of mine, Conrad Bosmans, is a digital marketer who landed an $18,000 consulting gig after one interview on a podcast episode. The host of the podcast (me) made him look like such an authority on his topic that one listener reached out immediately to procure Conrad's services. Of course, it helps that he's really good at what he does, and even better at explaining the value clearly.

Gus Christofi

Another example of how becoming a published author can transform a business is found with Constantis "Gus" Christofi. Gus owns Cosmos Heating & Cooling in Northern Virginia. He worked with me in 2016 to publish a book called *Insider Secrets of the HVAC Experts*. Gus recently shared with me that the book's publication has had a tremendous impact on his business. How? People don't question his pricing anymore. "I used to lose out if I gave a bid and another guy came in after me and offered it for $50 less, because the customers would go with him. But now they don't, because I'm the guy who wrote the book," he explained. But that's not all. In the HVAC business, most deals are worth $6,000–$12,000. He is closing multiple deals every month — at his desired price point — because his book cemented his subject matter expert status.

Other Everyday Examples

There's also Connie Fuksa of Foote Title Group in Maryland. She does a series of videos on YouTube called "Coffee with Connie," talking about issues related to real estate. And there's the case of Dr. Arian Mowlavi, a board-certified plastic surgeon in Laguna Beach, California. We're producing a series of recordings called the *High-Definition*

Liposuction Podcast. In less than thirty days our efforts have driven over $100,000 in new revenues for his practice.

Positioning yourself as a subject matter expert will dramatically increase your sales, no matter the size of your business or the industry you work in. But it doesn't work by magic.

How It Works

I'm going to give you a little bit of marketing theory here. Part of my subject matter expert status is based upon online courses I've published. I'm happy to report that, as of this writing, I have over 18,000 students in 165 countries enrolled in my courses.

As I mentioned previously, one of those courses is called *How to Build a Customer Factory.* You

The Customer Factory

Stranger	Suspect	Prospect	Customer	Client

The Marketing Assembly Line

Design Your Customer and then build a Marketing Assembly Line to produce them. The raw material we start with is targeted, qualified Strangers. The finished products we produce are A-List Customers and Clients. During the process, our product is refined through a series of stages called Stranger, Suspect, Prospect, Customer, Client.

The Marketing Assembly Line

If you envision this process as an assembly line, think of robot arms coming down out of the ceiling and applying different processes and tools to this prospect as they move down the line. Each tool being applied could be a radio ad, a billboard, a brochure, a live presentation or webinar, a business card or an in-person meeting. All of these things are marketing tools, applied sequentially over time.

In Digital Media Positioning, the robot arms are the helpful content you're providing your target client in the form of videos, audios, books and text. Your job is to use your free, valuable content to move them from "never heard of you" to "here's my credit card information."

Stranger

You first target your content at qualified Strangers. They've never heard of you, but you know enough about them to be sure that they fit your A-List Client profile. Little by little you drip relevant content on them, eventually breaking through to their consciousness enough that they become aware of your identity, and perhaps how you could solve their problem. They're beginning to know you, but they don't yet like you or trust you.

Suspect

Over time, a subset of your targeted Strangers will become aware that your name is Bob, and that you're a plumber. But they are highly suspicious of you and your motives relative to their need. Why are they suspicious? We're all suspicious any time a new marketing message breaks through our consciousness. We're inundated with hundreds of them on a daily basis, and most are of no relevance to us. Bob doesn't really understand my problem. He just wants to sell me something.

Prospect

Over time, some percentage of those Suspects will transform into Prospects, folks who are beginning to think that you *might* be a good solution for their problem, but they need more information. They like what they are learning about you, especially because your messaging is consistent and continuous, which breeds trust in your personal brand. You clearly understand their problem and have an immediate, effective and permanent solution, which has been validated by multiple third parties who are a lot like them.

Customer

An even smaller percentage of your Prospects will pull the trigger and buy something from you. This is a Golden Moment you must capitalize upon, ensuring that they have an exceptional first purchase experience. That will make it easier for them to move to the final stage of the marketing assembly line.

Client

A Customer is a first-time, one-time buyer of your product or service. A Client is an ongoing source of repeat and referral business. This is the ultimate goal, the finished product manufactured by The Customer Factory.

How Digital Media Positioning Supercharges the Marketing Assembly Line

Traditional marketing theory holds that the move from Stranger to Prospect is Marketing's job, while

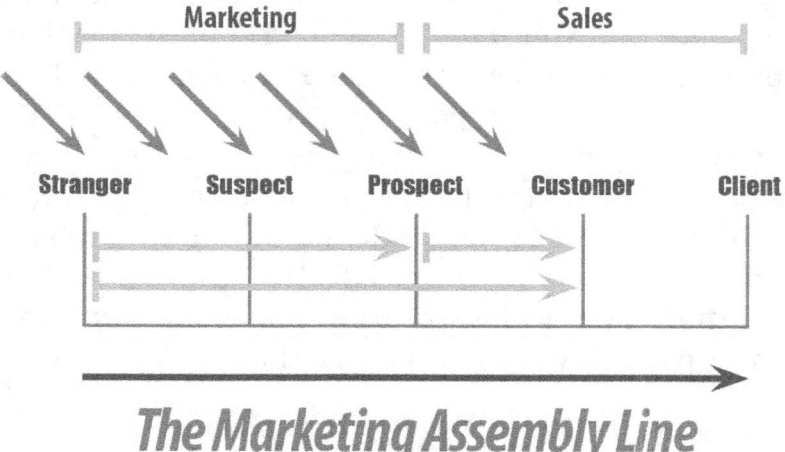

moving them from Prospect to Customer is Sales' job. Digital Media Positioning supports both of those segments of the customer's journey.

Your book, your videos, your podcast interviews and whitepapers all generate the Know, Like and Trust required to move your A-Lister from Stranger to Prospect. But your free information can also help seal the deal, by persuading a Prospect to buy today, and become your newest Customer.

Picture yourself in a sales presentation, in a boardroom or a kitchen. You say, "Mr. Jones, I appreciate you taking the time to meet with me today. Before we get started, instead of my business card, I want to give you a copy of my book, which shares a number of insights into the purchase you are considering making. Chapter Three directly addresses the service you are considering investing in, while Chapter One offers advice on how to work with service providers like myself, to ensure you make the right decision and enjoy the optimal outcome. Whichever company you choose to work with, I hope you will accept this book as my gift and make use of the information in it. Now, how can I help you today?" Could that help to close the deal? It does, every day.

Sometimes, Digital Media Positioning takes a Stranger all the way to Customer. That's what happened with that presentation I made in Florida. It's possible some of the people in attendance had seen my column in the magazine or heard of me somewhere through the printing industry. But I'd be willing to bet that the vast majority of the people that gave me $197 that day had never seen me before. The mere fact that I was on the stage and was introduced as the expert compelled them to respect what I had to say. But that wasn't all that was required to get them to buy a newsletter subscription. I gave them actual, actionable information that solved their problems and answered their questions.

Still Not Easy, But A Lot Easier

At that time, digital media was not yet available. So, positioning yourself as an expert used to be a very difficult thing to do. In Washington DC, for example, there were two daily newspapers, *The Post* and *The Star*. How are you going to get published in there? Pretty tough. Magazines were published monthly, one-thirtieth the frequency of newspapers, with even fewer pages available. How are you going to get in there? Again, pretty tough.

What about radio or television? Forget about it! It takes a big budget and a lot of time. You better have a great story to tell, a great publicist and $5,000 per month or more to invest. You say you want to get a book published? Are you kidding me? Most publishing houses printed more rejection letters than book titles by a ratio of 100:1.

Today, things are different. You can be in charge of all of this. You can publish instantaneously in video, audio, text or graphic format, and your content will remain available permanently. Contrast this with the 1990s. Just because you were featured in the print edition of the *New York Times* one day doesn't mean anyone in your A-List saw it. And if they didn't see it, it didn't happen. Today, your piece is on the Internet forever and people will find your content when they are searching for a solution to their problem.

Laser Targeting

You can also target exactly whom you want to speak to today. Back in the day, Barbara Corcoran's report was printed on the real estate page. That was pretty good targeting, but I'm sure there were a lot of people who read the real estate page who really weren't buying and selling real estate. And there was no actual way to track who read that article and who was moved by it. Today, you can speak to exactly and exclusively to your A-List target market, and watch how they react to what you have to say.

Chapter 3

Digital Media

What Is Digital Media?

Digital Media is what most marketing gurus call Content. And what they call Content Marketing, I refer to as Digital Media Positioning.

My definition of Digital Media is any free or paid answers to questions, or solutions to problems, that helps position you as the go-to Subject Matter Expert for your A-List target market. It can come in many forms: video, audio, social media, blogs, books, articles and so on.

The idea is that you give as much of your information as possible away for free. The goal is to get this reaction from your A-List clients: "This information is so good, they should charge for it." The goal is not for you to make a lot of money selling a lot of books, but for you to produce a book that sells a lot of you.

An important trap to avoid is the fear that people are going to rip-off your free content, put it to work without paying you or, worse yet, repackage it under their own brand and compete against you. Very few people would even consider taking such as step, and fewer still will actually do so. And, no matter who chooses to do what, you can't stop them anyway. No need to concern yourself with things you can't control. Cast your bread freely upon the water and the blessings will be returned to you manifold.

Probably the toughest piece of advice for people to follow — or even understand — is that you should give away all your best stuff. I'm talking about the information that makes people slap their forehead and say "Wow!" Don't worry that you have cherry-picked your best information and that they will be paying you later for that same advice or service, along with a lot of less fascinating services and direction. What you're trying to do here is position yourself as the go-to solution provider, not sell information.

I'll give you an example. Have you ever been to a movie and then realized later that all the best jokes, car crashes or action scenes were in the preview you saw on TV? That's not an accident. The producers give you all their best stuff to get you to come in and buy. You should take the same approach.

I want to stress here that Digital Media goes beyond digital to include print and live events. I include these in Digital Media because you can digitize all that content and repurpose it so you can give it away freely to a lot more people.

Just so you know, this book was taken from a digital recording of a live presentation I made to a room full of people. A lot of people had been saying to me, "Frank, you tell me I should have a book for my business. Well, where's *your* book for *your* business?" Here it is. I was essentially writing my book while giving the presentation, because I was recording it on video, which is the first type of Digital Media I'd like to talk about.

Video

Video takes many forms these days. There are "online accessible recordings," by which I generally mean YouTube videos. But there many other places where you can record video and post it where people can get to it: on your own website, on Facebook, LinkedIn, etc. It doesn't just have to be YouTube.

Presentations can be broadcast live, whether streaming live from an in-person seminar or on a desktop webinar. You can also do one-to-one desktop video communications, perhaps an instructional session or an interview via Skype or Zoom. If you're smart, you will record those presentations and repurpose them as well. The questions that someone asked you on a webinar or call are on other people's minds too. The answers you give today should be made available 24 hours a day forever to people you want to connect with. And they can be, if you take the steps to learn to produce, record and repurpose digital video.

Audio

Audio Content takes many forms, ranging from podcasting, whether as a host or guest, to audiobooks. I'm big on Audio Content, which is why I have been producing it in a variety of forms for decades, as a radio host, voice actor and podcast host. If you are inexperienced with audio production, I suggest you steer clear of creating your own podcast. Become a guest on other people's podcasts instead. You can be on multiple podcasts all around the world and reach tens of thousands of targeted listeners who are interested in exactly what it is that you have to say. You're going to be right inside their head — with them in their car, or in their ear buds while they're bicycling or exercising. It's as simple as getting on the phone or on a Skype call with the host, and then you'll have access to an audio recording of that interview forever, which you can then repurpose into text or even video.

Social

Digital Media can be produced and shared on Facebook, Instagram, LinkedIn, or any other platform available today or in the future. It includes articles, blogging, email, live streaming and online courses. The key is repurposing. You can do a live presentation, for example, and turn it into two months' worth of social media posts by having it recorded, transcribed, edited, chunked down, repurposed and scheduled.

I refer to email marketing as social media, because it's permission-based and interactive. Recipients can reply, forward or share on Facebook or elsewhere.

I'm not going to go into detail on online courses here, because there is just too much to talk about to include in a short book such as this one. But, as I told you, I've gathered over 18,000 students from around the world to my course platform. Talk about a way that you can become the "go-to" expert!

Print and PR

The development of on-demand printing and electronic publishing options has transformed the publishing industry. Your Digital Media can instantly take the form of an ebook, paperback, hard cover and audio formats, and be marketed worldwide on Amazon.com and Apple's iTunes Store.

Back in the 1990s, I would have to buy at least 1,000 books, maybe even 3,000 books, to get individual copies down to a unit cost that made any sense. Authors would order all these books, investing thousands (and sometimes tens of thousands) of dollars, only to have them piled up in their garage or attic where they would gather dust, mold and insects. Today you can have one copy of your book produced on demand, whether paperback or hard cover, at an incredibly low cost. Kindle has no duplication costs at all.

PR Content

Back in the day, when the only news outlets available were newspapers, magazines, radio and television, there was no 24-hour news cycle. Now there is. The existence of this insatiable monster means that news and publishing outlets are continuously looking for content. The probability of your story being picked up is greatly enhanced today, but it's not going to be picked up if you don't publish it.

In-Person Content

I include speaking opportunities, live sales presentations and networking meetings as a Digital Media category because, as I mentioned, you can capture them, digitize and repurpose them.

I never give any presentation without recording it. I don't care how short it is or how few people are in attendance. If I don't capture at least the audio portion, the content is lost forever. Any person not in the room at the time will never be able to benefit from the information I shared. And I will never be able to repurpose or publish it in order to help support my position of subject matter expert.

It literally hurts my feelings when a friend or colleague gives a presentation but fails to record it. Don't be that person.

Technical Requirements

Many people tell me that they "can't" record their presentations because they either don't have the necessary equipment or are too technically challenged to figure out how to use it. I get it. It's a lot to take in.

But let me assure you, everything you need is in your phone. It's an audio recorder and a high-quality video camera. It has an Internet connection and it came with headphones with a built-in microphone.

You *can* learn how to use these tools. All the training you need is available on YouTube. The question is, *will you* step out of your comfort zone and invest the time and emotional energy required to become proficient? Let's face it, it's not that you *can't* do it, it's that you *won't* do it. My hope is that I have been able to show how much you could benefit from learning how to produce your own Digital Media.

Chapter 4

Positioning Yourself with Digital Media

We've talked about Positioning. We've talked about Digital Media. Now, we're going to talk about how to Position yourself with Digital Media, which revolves around the Authority Wheel and how to use it to achieve subject matter expert status.

The Authority Wheel

The authority wheel is a six-spoke strategy diagram with your Message at the center. Each of the spokes — video, audio, social, publicity, publishing and in-person — depend on your ability to first craft a powerful, succinct central message. The effectiveness of your message is dependent upon your ability to answer three important questions with precision, power and passion.

Your Message

While the three questions below appear simple, answering them correctly will require a good deal of time and attention.

1. Who do you help?
2. What Problem do you solve?
3. What's your secret sauce?

Let's return to the examples in Chapter 2 for some insight into answering those questions.

What target market did Barbara Corcoran's firm help? Buyers and sellers of residential real estate on the island of Manhattan. What problem did she solve for her tribe? Ensuring that buyers didn't overpay, and sellers priced their listings correctly for rapid sale. What was her secret sauce? Her intimate knowledge of every comparable transaction as demonstrated by *The Corcoran Report.*

Who was Gary Vaynerchuk looking to help? People who enjoyed wine, but were not connoisseurs.

What problem did he solve? Uncovering vintages that delivered great taste at a reasonable price. What was his secret sauce? His *Wine Library TV* YouTube channel.

Who joins Dave Ramsey's tribe? People trying to get out of debt. What problem does he solve for them? Providing a workable path to rapid debt elimination. What is his secret sauce? His message is omnipresent through radio, Internet, books, live workshops and online courses.

Who does Dr. Arian Mowlavi help? Fit and attractive people looking to achieve something close to physical perfection. What problem does he solve for them? The ability to realize the perfect body shape and muscle definition they have not been able to achieve through rigorous exercise and stringent diet. What's his secret sauce? High-definition liposuction equipment, techniques and artistry.

Your Silver Bullet Tagline

Having answered those questions for yourself, you have one last task in order to maximize the power of your message: create your Silver Bullet tagline.

This is a powerful concept public speaking coach extraordinaire Neil Gordon recently introduced to me.

"The Silver Bullet of your message is a single sentence that pairs up the action your prospect must take and the beneficial outcome they will receive."

Among many examples he gives is that of a woman who gave a short presentation to charitable organizations explaining why they should donate to her foundation, which provides books and adult readers to share with hospitalized children. Her Silver Bullet message? Literacy Can Heal. Bang! The money poured in.

The Message Onion

Once you have achieved absolute clarity and your Message has found its Silver Bullet expression, you must be prepared to deliver it in ever-expanding levels of detail, depending upon the amount of time and attention your listener has granted you. I call this your Message Onion because there are layers to this message, each with more detail than the last. You should be prepared to deliver your message effectively at all of these levels:

The **Seed** is your tagline or mission statement: One Silver Bullet sentence.

Your **Elevator Pitch** describes your service and target market in 60 seconds or less.

Your **Spotlight Presentation** is a five-minute networking breakfast talk.

Your **Shark Tank Speech** is a ten-minute concentrated investor presentation.

Your **TED Talk** is 18-20 minutes that can be transcribed into a short Kindle.

Your **Keynote Presentation** is 45-60 minutes of anecdotes and examples that can also be repurposed as a printed pocketbook and about 90 days of social content.

Your **Seminar** is three hours of intense instruction with role-play and activities that can also be repurposed into a paperback book and about six months of social content.

Your **Boot Camp** is two days with enough content create a hardcover book and at least twelve months of daily social media content.

After you've discovered your Silver Bullet, next begin crafting a 30-second elevator speech. As part of my radio career, I wrote and produced a lot of 30-second spots. Stating the problem, presenting the solution, and calling to action in less than 30 seconds is exceedingly difficult. It takes a lot of work, focused attention discipline. I recommend it to you because it forces you to get down to the real essence of what it is that you do. Who do you help? What problem do you solve? Why should anybody care? If you can't answer those questions in less than a minute, there's a problem.

The Power of Focused Messaging

As you will learn as you work to build your Message Onion, successful message crafting is tough. So, is it really worth the effort? I would argue no other task is more worthy of your attention if your goal is to attract nothing but A-List Clients.

About three years ago, I met with a lady who had asked me to help her launch her new business. I said, "Okay. Who do you help, what problem do you solve, and what's your secret sauce?" After two hours, I had yet to hear the answer to even one of those questions. It was clear to me that she didn't have a business model, just a nebulous dream. All my questions did was frustrate and anger her. And her answers — or inability to answer — was having the same effect on me. We did not work together, and she has yet to launch that business.

So, it's important you get focused. In Martin Saenz's case, he had a narrow focus. He wasn't just talking about the broad category of "real estate." He wasn't even talking about the somewhat narrower topic of "real estate investing." He homed in on investing in distressed mortgage notes, an ultra-specific industry within the real estate investing niche.

Another example is a friend of mine named Stephen Kann, whose book *Microcap Magic* I published in 2015. His message isn't just about investing, or even just investing in stocks. He has a specific focus: investing in small, publicly traded companies with very low trading volumes.

Dr. Arian Mowlavi is the plastic surgeon I mentioned earlier who does elective liposuction. But he doesn't just do liposuction, which is a niche within cosmetic surgery. He focuses on an even tighter sub-niche called *high-definition* liposuction.

The more targeted your message, the more responsive your target market will be. I know it's counterintuitive, but it is absolutely the fact. Highly successful businesspeople understand this secret and A-List Clients are attracted to laser-focused messages like moths to a flame.

Write the Back Cover

Another tactic you can try if you're struggling to compose your 30-second pitch is to write the back cover of your future book. I was taught many years ago that, when writing my first non-fiction how-to book, that the first and most important page you need to write is the back cover. The back cover presents the Big Promise of the book, the transformational experience that will accrue to the reader who has the wisdom to purchase and consume it.

In effect, the back cover starts with a headline that expresses the equivalent of "In This Book You Will Learn," followed by six to ten bullet-pointed short sentences communicating powerful value propositions. This is the exercise I have every new author do first. How will your readers benefit? What is the big idea of this book? These are the same questions you must be able to answer clearly about your business if you wish to attract nothing but A-List Clients.

Record Something

Now you're ready to start producing some Digital Media to support the Authority Positioning you're seeking to create. Take the back cover you just wrote, get out your phone, put on your ear buds, turn on the voice memo app and start talking. (Go ahead! I dare you.)

Start reading the bullet points and explaining them to an imaginary A-List Prospect. Listen to the recording. You hate the way your voice sounds on tape? Welcome to the club. I have never met anyone who did not say that to me. Forget about that and turn your attention to the substance of your words. Which points did you express well? Which did you struggle supporting with your explanation? Which of those just need more work and which do you need to jettison?

Lather, rinse, repeat until you are feeling very good about your messaging. Then send your polished recording to a transcription service to see how your words look on paper. Congratulations! You've just repurposed your first piece of Digital Media, which can now be used to start your Authority Positioning process.

The next step is to get yourself interviewed, or interview someone else. Have you ever heard of Napoleon Hill? He wrote a little book called *Think and Grow Rich*. How did he do that? By interviewing many of the most successful, wealthy people of his day. He wasn't rich. He knew nothing about wealth building. But interviewing those people and publishing his findings has permanently positioned him as an expert on the topic.

Repurposing Content

Just as you have recorded your verbal description of the back cover of your book, I audiotape every presentation I give. This book is the result of one such recording, taken from a 53-minute presentation I made in August 2017, which was then transcribed and edited into the final product you are reading right now. No matter what you start with; audio, video, text, webinar, blog post, podcast, interview — you name it — that content can be repurposed at least five different ways and then published globally to support your subject matter expert status.

The way I help new authors write their first book is by drawing it out of them through a series of interviews. We write the back cover and then structure the table of contents based upon the Big Promise of the book. Each chapter addresses a high-level problem their A-List Prospects face. Next, we identify five to eight frequently asked questions — or should be frequently asked questions — that examine that high-level problem in detail and provide specific solutions and steps to take.

We then conduct remote desktop video interviews using a platform called Zoom.us. I sit at my desk and the author sits at his. Using webcams and microphones we cover each chapter as a single interview. I ask the simple, powerful questions we've designed and the author speaks at length, solving problems for his tribe. Those video recordings are edited and their audio tracks are extracted. The audio is then transcribed and professionally edited. The resulting content (audio, video, text) can then be repurposed on an almost unlimited basis, making it available instantly and permanently to A-List Prospects around the world.

In the case of Martin Saenz, we shot 11 videos, in which I interviewed him about different topics related to his note investing business. We extracted 11 audios from those and then we created the 11 chapters in his book from the transcribed audio files.

Now Martin has a video library of 11 videos, an audio library of 11 audios and a published Amazon bestseller that is available in paperback, Kindle and audiobook. He's taken this same information and repurposed it into a two-day workshop for which he charges $2,000 per ticket. The result of his successful Digital Media Positioning is that he also has a waiting list of people who will to pay him $25,000 for six months of direct mentoring. The first six months of this program have already generated over $100,000 in new revenue directly attributable to his new position in the minds of his tribe.

Here are some more repurposing ideas:

As I mentioned previously, I have a 10-hour online course called *How to Build a Customer Factory*. I'm in the process of repurposing it by turning it into a book. Ten hours of transcribed audio is going to produce one thick book! I am also turning it into a two-day live workshop.

I work with a client who sends out a weekly email to about 4,000 people. Each week we also repurpose the email content into a tweet, a Facebook post, a blog post, and a LinkedIn Pulse article. As of this writing we have followed this system religiously for 61 consecutive weeks and the impact on their business has been nothing short of amazing.

Another Authority Wheel: Repurposing

At the beginning of this chapter, I showed you the Authority Wheel with Message at the center and the different Digital Media through which you can express your message represented by spokes. Now we are going to change it slightly to become The Repurposing Wheel, which places Recording at the center of six spokes: Book, Course, Podcast, Video, Email and Social Media. But you could take any one of the spokes and move it to the center and then repurpose it at least five ways. Any piece of Content can be repurposed provided that it has been turned into Digital Media.

Think your presentation is too short or your live audience too small to warrant the hassle of capturing a digital audio recording? Think again.

I have a book that debuted at #1 on the Amazon bestseller list entitled *Unlocking The M Cube*. I

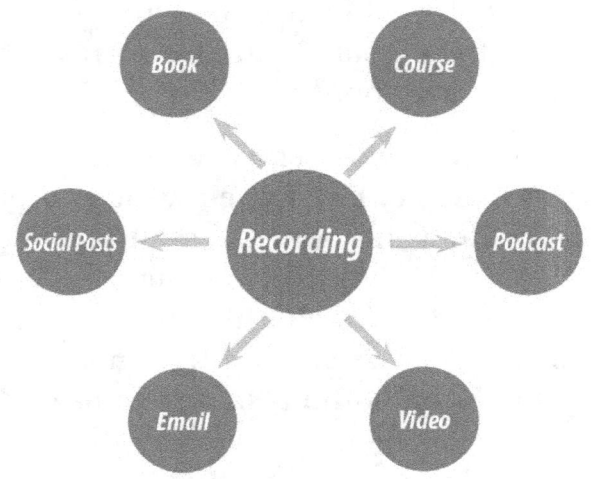

The Authority Wheel

wrote this book in 10 minutes by audio recording my BNI keynote presentation with an iPhone. I specifically created the slide deck to support this objective, got up in front of the group and spoke for ten minutes. Afterward, I converted the audio recording into a book, using the slide deck as an outline for the chapters and subheads and filling in the gaps with the edited transcription.

In addition to a Kindle edition, I also published it as a 68-page 5" x 8" book. You can read it from cover to cover in 30 minutes. Think that's too short to be taken seriously? *Of Mice and Men, The Art of War* and *As A Man Thinketh* are all about the same length. Just do it.

I also combined the audio recording with the slide deck to create a short video. Now people around the world can consume that information in whatever medium they prefer: audio, video or text.

Chapter 5

Attracting Nothing But A-list Clients with Digital Media Positioning

We've talked about Positioning. We've talked about Digital Media. We've talked about capturing and repurposing Digital Media to position yourself as the authority. Now we're going to talk about Attracting Nothing But the A-list clients you've identified with Digital Media Positioning.

Having read and implemented the information up to this point, you now have a clear, laser-focused message. You know exactly who your A-list Prospects are, what problem you solve for them and what your secret sauce is. You are publishing helpful free content. From your A-List's perspective, you're starting to look pretty dang attractive!

The Four Attraction Zones

There are four zones where you can attract A-list Clients with Digital Media Positioning:

1. Online, using SEO, Search Engine Marketing, Social Media and targeted ads
2. Speaking opportunities

3. Networking meetings
4. Sales presentations.

The Online Zone

There are a lot of Internet Marketing Gurus with a lot of systems for selling products and services online, but few are targeted at selling an individual. The most direct and understandable online Authority Positioning process I've ever seen is Voice-Activated Marketing from K. Conrad Bosmans of Laguna Beach, California.

The first step in Conrad's process is digital media content creation. Next, you publish it that content where your customers are most likely to find it. Then you promote it in three specific ways, leading to the last step where respondents go into sales funnels directly related to the content they responded to.

The result is a continuous online flow of A-List Prospects consuming your content, providing you their contact information and giving you permission to continue to drip on them until they either buy, die, or opt out. Explaining the details would require five books this size, so I suggest visiting Bosman's website, vamomedia.com.

The Speaking Zone

Speaking engagements are powerful opportunities to attract A-List Clients. The two secrets are 1) landing the right opportunities in front of the right audiences and 2) having a systematic way to turn butts in seats into prospects in a database and dollars in the bank.

The number one thing that will attract more A-List speaking opportunities is an exceedingly clear message. There's an old expression from radio that says you want people to either turn up the volume or change the channel. Your clear message instantly informs the listener whether they should invest additional time in hearing you out. Some speaking bookers and show producers will have absolutely no interest in your message. That's a good thing. It's important to repel them quickly so that you're not wasting your time presenting your message to disinterested audiences. Other bookers and producers will wonder where you've been hiding their entire lives and be anxious to get you in front of their tribe as soon as possible because your message represents a unique solution to a common problem for their audience.

Once you're in front of your ideal audience, give it all up like one of your favorite movie trailers. Don't hold anything back. Give people all your best information, and give it to them for free. That's all a part of you becoming that trusted, generous educator and sincere advocate for their success.

Converting Butts in Seats into Prospects and Clients

Your objective in landing speaking engagements is to initiate and begin to nurture client relationships.

If you do a good job on the stage, your audience will love you – until the ether wears off and they are entranced by the next shiny object. So, it is critical that you have a system in place to capture their contact information and/or sell them something before they leave the room.

The co-founders of the training firm Color Accounting International, give free seminars at venues large and small around the world. Many of these events are put on by huge organizations such as the Society for Human Resource Management (SHRM) and the Association for Talent Development (ATD). These associations love having great content presented at their conferences, but jealously guard their attendee lists and dislike speakers selling their wares from the stage. How can a speaker turn attendees at these conferences into clients or opt-ins without running afoul of their hosts? By getting creative.

Shortly after Color Accounting became my client, we created a simple system through which they could gather contact information from attendees during and directly after every presentation via text message. Three times during the presentation; near the beginning, around the middle and at the very end, our speaker will say, "I have brought five printed copies of our bestselling book as gifts for those who are brave enough to approach a microphone and ask a question. But we want everyone to have a free digital copy available by download. Just text SHRM17 to 74747 and we'll send you the link."

About 40% of the attendees will send the text from their phone while they're in the room. Our system instantly replies to their text with a request that they reply with their email address, so we can email them the link. About 80% of the original 40% provide their email address via reply text. If there are 1,000 people in the room, we have just added 320 of those most engaged with our message to our email list. After they receive the link to the book we put them into a five-day autoresponder series that presents a series of short videos. After that, they go into our weekly newsletter list. This is a tremendous improvement over walking away with business cards from the 5–6 people who are able to speak with the presenter before they must leave to attend the next seminar.

Much of what we implemented for Color Accounting, I learned in the 1990s from a great speaker named Roger Dawson, who moved me to fork over $297 for his package of information about negotiation skills at one of his seminars. On a side note, if you have any concern about repurposing information because the exact same information in your video is also in your book and in your presentation, this example should disabuse you of that fear.

Roger stood up in front of a group of about a thousand of us printers for a two-hour presentation at the Hyatt hotel in downtown Chicago. "Before I get started," he said, "I want to let you know that I am not being paid a penny to present today. Your trade association paid for first-class airfare, a nice hotel room and a great steak dinner. Other than that, I'm going to be walking out of here with nothing unless you buy some of my stuff in the back of the room at the end of the presentation. So, I'd like to make a deal with you. I'm going to give you all kinds of great information for free, and all I ask for in exchange is that you allow me to also share three commercial messages, of which this is the first. Is everybody okay with that? Great. Let me get started…"

He then went on to deliver an hour filled with fire hose quantities of valuable information about negotiating skills. He paused, drank a couple of sips of water, and said, "Here's commercial message #2. You all have order forms in front of you and you can see that if you were to buy everything on the list — my hardcover book, my audiotapes, my workbook and video series — the total price would be $1,245. I want every one of you to get out a pen, and circle that number, $1,245." Then he presented his second hour of compelling, actionable information regarding how to make more money at almost every turn by becoming a more effective negotiator.

At the conclusion of his presentation, every person in the room was dying to find out what the final pitch was going to be and whether or not we would be able to afford the privilege of buying his wares. The great man paused for a long moment, and then said, "This is my third and final commercial message. Thank you for your indulgence. Please put your pen in your hand and locate the number $1,245 that you had previously circled. Use your pen to strike through that number. Now prepare to write another number below it. For everyone in this room right now, I will let you go home with this complete package of information for only $297."

At first the room was hushed but then a murmuring began to arise as folks asked their neighbor what they thought about that price point. Nobody budged from their chair, until Roger added, "We were only able to bring ten complete sets with us, which, of course, will go to the first ten people who approach our back table." At that people began jumping from their seats and scurrying to the back of the room.

When it was clear that the ten complete sets had already been spoken for, the great showman added, "It appears our inventory has already been exhausted. But for everyone who completes their order form and has their credit card processed in the next 20 minutes, I guarantee your order will ship today from our California office, and probably get to your home or office just about the same time you return from this conference."

At that point it was virtual pandemonium in the room. When the dust cleared, my estimation was that, in addition to first class travel, meals and accommodation, Roger Dawson walked out of the room with over $24,000 in sales. Not a bad haul for two hours work. And the team at the back of the room? They were employees of the trade association Dawson had trained that morning to support him at no charge. All part of the original deal he cut to present.

Repurposing Anxiety

When I got home and opened the box I found that the hardcover book had the same information in it that Dawson had given us in his presentation. The video series was the same speech I'd just watched, but it was converted into video tapes. The audio package was the same speech on audio tapes. And the same went for the workbook. It was all the same information repurposed 12 different ways. But I will tell you, to this day, I am a much better negotiator than I was before I saw Roger Dawson in Chicago. Every person consumes, comprehends and retains information differently. And the more ways and more times you consume the same message, the better you will comprehend it, retain it and confidently act upon it. I have received my $297 investment back many times per year from that information and all the ways I cemented it into my mind. Have no fear of repurposing your information. You are doing your tribe a favor.

I recently did a Google search on "Roger Dawson" to see what his marketing and content look like 25 years later. He has a book called *Secrets of Power Negotiating: Updated for the 21st Century*. He has niched his message down into other books for specific audiences, with topics on negotiating power for salespeople, negotiating power for real estate, negotiating your next raise, etc. A lot of people do it the other way. They start with the small topic, like negotiating for real estate, and then they ladder up to wider and wider groups.

In my case, I have the book you are reading, *Digital Media Positioning: The Art and Science of Attracting Nothing But A-list Clients,* which will then be niched-down for titles such *as Digital Media Positioning for Attorneys, Digital Media Positioning for Medical Professionals*, and so on.

The Networking Zone

Until you get serious about attracting A-List Clients at networking meetings, you're wasting your time. There's no point in getting up early, grabbing 40 business cards and driving across town to give a 30-second elevator pitch to a roomful of strangers without a plan. You might as well stay home under the covers.

Before you even walk into the room, you should have a clear objective in mind of what you're trying to accomplish. Think about it the night before and on the drive over to the meeting. Know who your A-list prospects are. If possible, scan the member list ahead of time looking for A-Listers. When you see one, zero in on them. Don't think about all the other people you may want to talk to, just give all your attention to that one person. If you come out of there having initiated a single new relationship that you can potentially nurture into an A-List Client, that meeting was a success.

Walk up to them and say something like, "Hi, Joe, I'm really interested in what you said about architecture. I didn't know there was a firm like yours in the area. Tell me a little bit more about what you do." Joe, hopefully, will reply with a good elevator speech about what he does and what problem he solves.

Now you'll be able to introduce what *you* do, tailoring it for Joe's business. Tell him who you are and what you do for architects looking to solve a specific problem. But don't talk too much. Maybe five minutes maximum. As soon as you get back to your office, send him a thank you email and a thank you card, which he will receive in a few days in the mail. Add him to your email list so you will remain top of mind. Send him some of your free content related to what you two had discussed. Send him other people's content that you think is appropriate.

Even more powerful is to introduce yourself by handing Joe a copy of your book, using it as your calling card. Autograph it for him on the spot and point out any chapter or section you think he would get the most value from, saving him from agreeing to read the whole book. Again, follow up with a thank you email and card and send free content featuring your expertise in solving a specific problem for him.

The Sales Zone

I have previously described how you can use your book as a calling card to take control at the beginning of any sales presentations and quickly elevate yourself above the noise of your competition. Another effective technique is Rich Harshaw's Prepositioning Package, where you FedEx an autographed copy of your book along with a personal note ahead of your sales presentation. Here are a couple more creative applications.

Mike Koenigs is a well-known Internet marketer who preaches many of the same practices I do. When boarding a plane a couple of years ago, Mike happened to see that Richard Dreyfuss was sitting in the first-class section. After he got to his seat in coach, but before the plane took off, Koenigs got on his phone and did an Internet search for Richard Dreyfuss. He learned that Dreyfuss had created a foundation to support the teaching of Civics in American public schools, but was having a hard time raising money for it.

Koenigs always carries copies of his own book, *Publish & Profit*, so he pulled one out and wrote inside the front cover, "Mr. Dreyfuss, I have an idea for you about how you can raise money for your foundation. On page 43 is something you can use right now. Text me at 987-654-3212 with any questions." Politely approaching Dreyfuss' seat in-flight, Koenigs said, "It's an honor to meet you Mr. Dreyfuss. I have an idea for you about how you can raise money for your foundation. It's on page 43. I hope I haven't intruded."

The men had no further interaction on the plane. Upon landing, the first-class section disembarked first, while Koenigs and the rest of the folks in coach waited their turn. There was no way for Koenigs to catch Dreyfuss as he left the plane. But, as he was walking through the airport Dreyfuss called Koenigs on his cell phone to ask a few questions. They ended up sitting down and having lunch, and now they're doing business together.

You can also use your book — or any book for that matter — to leapfrog a gatekeeper and get a package directly to your A-List Prospect, using another Mike Koenigs trick. Purchase the book at retail on Amazon.com and choose the gift wrap option during check out. Write a short personal message (255 characters max) that follows Koenigs "I have an idea that can solve your problem. Read page 43." Include a bit.ly URL to a personalized video for extra impact.

Because the box arrives in Amazon packaging addressed to the A-List Prospect, there is a high probability that the gatekeeper won't even open it, much less block it. If they do open it, they will find a gift inside, also difficult to keep from the boss. I'm not implying that every time you do this it will turn into a magic phone call from your prospect. But, if you are an Amazon Prime member, for the retail price of your book plus $4.95 for gift wrapping, it is a creative way to break through the noise of your competition and into the consciousness of your A-List Prospect.

Sales is a tough game, and nothing will guarantee a 100% closing rate. But having a published book in your toolbox, and knowing how and when to use it, can quickly increase your closing percentage by 50% or more. If your average sales price approaches or exceeds $10,000, this is a tool that will pay for itself in just a few weeks and continue to make you a mint for years to come.

Conclusion

I've covered quite a bit of strategy and many different tactics in this book. You may be thinking, "I can't do this! It's too technical! It sounds like a lot of work! I don't know where to start!"

The fact is that you can do this, it's just a question of whether or not you will. If you continue to do what you've always done, you will continue to get what you've always gotten. The change must start with you. I have shown you what to do, and why. Only you can take action.

By hesitating, you're not just hurting yourself; you're withholding your energy, love, knowledge and wisdom from the world. All the help you could be offering is locked in your heart and mind. The only people who can benefit from it are those who have the opportunity to stand right in front of you. By taking the actions necessary to implement what you've learned in this book, you remove the bushel covering your light and let it shine upon the entire world.

Where To Start

Define your message with those three questions: Who do you help? What problem do you solve? What's unique about you? Then identify who your A-listers are. Spend some real time with that. Get specific. Then build your Authority Wheel, with your Message in the middle and the different ways you will express your message, such as audio, video, text, etc., spelled out in the spokes.

Don't get overwhelmed by the technical aspects of this. You can do it. Start by recording a 10-minute audio using the "back of the book" strategy I mentioned before. Write the back cover of your future book, using the bullets as a structure. Then "teach" it back to yourself by speaking to your smart phone using the built-in voice memo app. Have that recording transcribed by humans at Rev.com for one dollar per minute, or by robots at Trint.com (25 cents per minute) or Temi.com (10 cents per minute).

Then get your transcription edited. Hire a professional editor or edit it yourself. It's only 10 minutes of content. You can afford to pay for that much editing. Turn the edited transcription into a blog post or an email. Post it on social media. Put it into your email signature. Use it to create a PDF whitepaper that you can forward to someone after a networking meeting or a sales call.

Sales guru Grant Cardone says that it's your duty, obligation and responsibility to be as successful in business as you can possibly be. The way I look at it, the more people you help, the more successful you will be. So it is your duty, obligation and responsibility to *help* as many people as you can. I've just shown you how you.

I'll leave you with this final thought from Seth Godin, author of *Tribes*. The subtitle is *We Need You to Lead Us*. This is how I want you to think about your A-list Clients. They're thinking, "We need some help here. Lead us."

Remember, life's too short to keep putting things off. You don't want to end up on the porch in a rocking chair thinking, "Gee, I wish I would have published that online course, or my book, when I had the chance, but I was too afraid." Do something you believe in, and you will leave a legacy that will last forever.

Afterword

During the six months between August 2017, when I first prepared and delivered the 53-minute presentation from which this book was drawn, and February 2018, when it was published, a number of additional Digital Media Positioning ideas and nuances have been revealed to me.

A-List Clients Enrich Your Life

Just as S-Listers frustrate you and sap your energy, A-Listers inspire you and fill you with energy. Working with A-Listers also allows you to observe them first-hand, watch what they do and how they do it, listen to what they say, see how they conduct themselves and how they respond to both adversity and triumph. Success leaves clues, but only if you're looking for them.

You can also learn a tremendous amount from your A-List Clients about their area of expertise. I knew nothing about investing in distressed mortgage notes before meeting Martin Saenz, but now I know more about the topic than 95% of the population. He has similarly schooled me on what is required to market goods and services to the Federal Government.

After working with Jason Osser, CPA, on his book, *Riding QuickBooks to The Promised Land*, I decided to implement the program in my own firm and was able to quickly get up to speed, inputting data and generating powerful reports. I also learned about investing in small, publicly traded companies from Steve Kann (*Microcap Magic*), dog training from Russ Crager (*What Your Dog Is Trying To Tell You*), home improvement from Jeremiah Davies (*Your Northern Virginia Home*) and heating and cooling systems from Gus Christofi (*Insider Secrets Of The HVAC Experts*).

The sooner you stop working with complainers and skinflints and begin working exclusively with successful people who understand abundance mentality, the better for you and your mental health.

Why It's Okay to Charge A-Listers a Lot More for the Same Product or Service

Subsequent to writing the bulk of this book, I joined Frank Kern's Inner Circle, a very pricy membership site that provides guidance to people creating and marketing information products. Kern is the highest-paid copywriter in this industry and has achieved near-legend status among infopreneurs like myself.

While watching one of his video lessons, I was struck by something he said rather off-handedly. Paraphrasing here, his thought was something like, "The same solution is worth one hundred times more to a guy generating a million dollars a year than it is to a guy generating $10,000."

If one of Kern's insights could increase the sales of a single information product by 100%, the million-dollar producer might see a $100,000 bump in revenue while the $10,000 earner would only see a $1,000 increase. If access to Kern's solution costs $5,000, which one of those two is more likely to buy it?

Your reaction to this story might be, "Yeah, but there are a lot more little guys out there than big guys." If you are still reacting this way after reading this book, you have completely missed the point. Kern is making millions by using the Value Ladder to offer beneficial information to every budget.

Perry Marshall and the Pareto Principle

Another thought leader I reengaged with after finishing this book was Perry Marshall, author of *80/20 Sales & Marketing*. As I read his audiobook for a second time, I realized how many of the ideas I share here had been influenced by my first reading. Marshall sees the 80/20 rule as a fractal law of Nature that applies to everything from Marketing to the veins on the back or your hand.

I'm sure Perry would agree with my premise that you should be focusing your marketing efforts on A-Listers, that 20% of clients who bring you 80%

or your revenue or profits. But he would take it one step farther — or perhaps two or three. What about the 20% of that 20%? These are the 4% of your clients that bring you 64% of your profits. Or the next group: the 1% who bring you 50%? These people are fifty times more valuable than the average client on your list. Not 50% more valuable, 5,000% more valuable.

I am now reviewing my current client list — A-Listers all — looking for those four-percenters and one-percenters. I'm applying my own methodology of determining what makes them different, where their pain points are and how I can provide evermore focused solutions. And I'm creating A-List Avatars to learn where to find more just like them.

That's All Folks

As with any creative work, at some point the writer or artist must call a halt to any further input. The newspaper is put to bed. The film is put in the can. This book is going to press.

I will continue to post ideas and resources on my Digital Media Positioning blog, as well as on social platforms including Twitter, Facebook and LinkedIn. I invite you to join me there to share your thoughts and reactions.

About the Author

Frank Felker with Social Media Marketing students at Fairfax Academy in Northern Virginia

Frank Felker has more than 40 years' experience starting, running and growing small businesses.

During that time, he has come to know hundreds of entrepreneurs as friends and peers, and has worked with thousands more as clients, students and seminar attendees. From his first day behind the counter of his family's copy shop, he has struggled to understand the secret that separates that small fraction of small business owners who thrive and succeed from the vast majority who struggle and fail.

At this point in his career, Frank's focus is entrepreneurial education — sharing his experience to help others design the life of their dreams by creating and running successful businesses.

Over 20,000 entrepreneurs from 165 countries have enrolled in his online small business courses and he has taught thousands more at live events across the United States, in Britain, Germany and Brazil.

Frank holds a Bachelor of Science in Economics from George Mason University, where he was a member of the Omicron Delta Epsilon International Economics Honor Society and the GMU Forensics Team (competitive public speaking), where he earned over 30 awards, including Fifth in the Nation in Impromptu Speaking.

A best-selling author and the host of the Radio Free Enterprise podcast, Frank Felker is the father of two children, Jessica and James.

www.ingramcontent.com/pod-product-compliance
Lightning Source LLC
Chambersburg PA
CBHW071058240526
45471CB00016B/2153